CONTENTS

BOOKS

PUBLISHED BY PEDIGREE BOOKS LIMITED
THE OLD RECTORY, MATFORD LANE, EXETER EX2 4PS

£6.99

DC2

BATMAN™

CODE RED-- CELL BLOCK A--!

--HELLGRAMMITE'S BUSTED OUT!

THAT SURE BEATS LISTENING TO THE WARDEN DODGE QUESTIONS ABOUT *PRISON REFORM*, eh, DREW?

STEP ASIDE, RYDER-- THIS IS *MY* STORY!

HELLGRAMMITE'S ONE TOUGH CUSTOMER! THE GUARDS ARE GOING TO NEED *HELP*--

--THE KIND OF HELP ONLY *I* CAN PROVIDE.

I'VE GOT A FREAKISH STEW OF CHEMICALS IN MY BLOOD, THANKS TO AN ENCOUNTER WITH *THE JOKER*--AND A SWAN DIVE INTO A VAT OF INDUSTRIAL WASTE!

THIS PATCH KEEPS IT UNDER CONTROL. ONCE I REMOVE IT, I BECOME--

"THE --CREEPER

MY BODY'S NOW ALMOST *INDESTRUCTIBLE*-- ALL I HAVE TO WORRY ABOUT IS MY *MIND!*

ON THE OTHER HAND, A LITTLE *INSANITY* CAN BE *FUN!*

HAHAHAHAHAH HAHAHAHAHAHA

KRACK

IT'S NOT *YOU* I'M AFTER, CLOWN -- IT'S *BATMAN!*

OUCHIE!

BUT IF I *EVER* *SEE YOU* *AGAIN,* I'LL *KILL YOU!*

NOW *THERE'S* A REASON TO GET UP IN THE MORNING...

LOOK AT 'IM GO! WE'LL *NEVER* CATCH HIM!

I'D SWEAR I SAW *THE CREEPER* A MINUTE AGO!

I'LL BET *HE* HELPED HELLGRAMMITE ESCAPE!

MY HEALING POWER'S KICKING IN -- GOTTA PULL MYSELF TOGETHER AND GET OUT OF HERE!

ONE OF THESE DAYS, I MAY NOT HAVE THE WILLPOWER TO TURN MYSELF BACK INTO *JACK RYDER!*

MADNESS CAN BE *SEDUCTIVE!*

WHERE'VE YOU BEEN, RYDER? DON'T TELL ME YOU'VE MISSED *ANOTHER* STORY!

THE DAY I LET *YOU* DEFINE WHAT'S A GOOD STORY IS THE DAY I QUIT BEING A *REPORTER,* DREW.

"--OR *WHOEVER* HELPED HIM ESCAPE!"

WHERE IS THAT LOUSY *BUG*?

THEY SAY THAT PATIENCE IS A VIRTUE.

YAAH!

HOW CAN SOMETHING SO *BIG* MOVE SO SILENTLY?!

IT'S ABOUT TIME YOU GOT HERE! I WAS BEGINNING TO THINK--

--THAT I'D FORGOTTEN OUR *BARGAIN*? DON'T WORRY.

YOU FREED ME FROM *PRISON*! IT'LL BE MY PLEASURE TO RETURN THE FAVOR--

--BY *DESTROYING* *BATMAN*!

BUT FIRST, THERE'S SOMETHING ELSE I MUST TAKE CARE OF...

HEY! STOP! LET ME GO!

YOU NEEDN'T BOTHER TO *STRUGGLE*--MY COCOON FIBERS ARE STRONGER THAN *STEEL*!

... UNTIL NEXT WEEK THIS IS JACK RYDER--

--AND THAT'S THE *TRUTH!*

:SPLUT!:

NICE WORK, MIKE.

THANKS, MR. RYDER--YOU TOO.

RYDER!

WHAT KIND OF A SIGN-OFF WAS *THAT?!* YOU GOTTA *GRAB* THE VIEWERS-- GIVE 'EM A REASON TO TUNE IN NEXT WEEK!

I *GIVE* THEM A REASON--MY JOURNALISTIC INTEGRITY!

HA! MAYBE THAT'LL LURE A FEW *PBS* WATCHERS!

BE *BOLD! SEXY!* MAKE 'EM WANNA *KILL* ANYTHING THAT COMES BETWEEN THEM AND THEIR TV!

DAN DREW IS *DESTROYING* US, RATINGS-WISE! JUST LOOK AT THIS AD!

YOU KNOW WHERE EVERY TV IN GOTHAM WILL BE TUNED NEXT WEEK--UNLESS *YOU* BEAT HIM TO THE PUNCH!

NEXT WEEK: DAN DREW'S HOT COPY

?

BATMAN UNMASKED! WATCH IT! GCSD

YOU WANT *ME* TO UNMASK *BATMAN?*

YOU WANT TO GET TO THE *TRUTH,* DON'T YOU?! WE CAN'T HAVE *COSTUMED VIGILANTES* RUNNING LOOSE! THEY'RE A *MENACE!*

BESIDES, IF *DREW* CAN DO IT, *YOU CAN-- RIGHT?!*

AND IF YOU'RE NOT UP TO IT, MAYBE I'LL HAVE TO FIND SOMEBODY WHO *IS!*

hmm... MAYBE THERE *IS* SOME TRUTH IN WHAT HE'S SAYING.

AS THE *CREEPER*, I'VE COME DANGEROUSLY CLOSE TO *LOSING CONTROL!* MAYBE I *AM* A MENACE--

--AND WHAT IF *BATMAN'S* THE SAME WAY?!

AND IT WOULD BE A HECK OF A STORY! I'D HATE TO BE SCOOPED BY THAT HACK *DREW!*

DID YOU HEAR THE LATEST? THEY SAY *RYDER'S* ON HIS WAY OUT--

--AND MANAGEMENT'S OFFERING *DAN DREW* BIG BUCKS TO *REPLACE HIM!*

I'M NOT SURPRISED, CONSIDERING RYDER'S *RATINGS* LATELY.

15

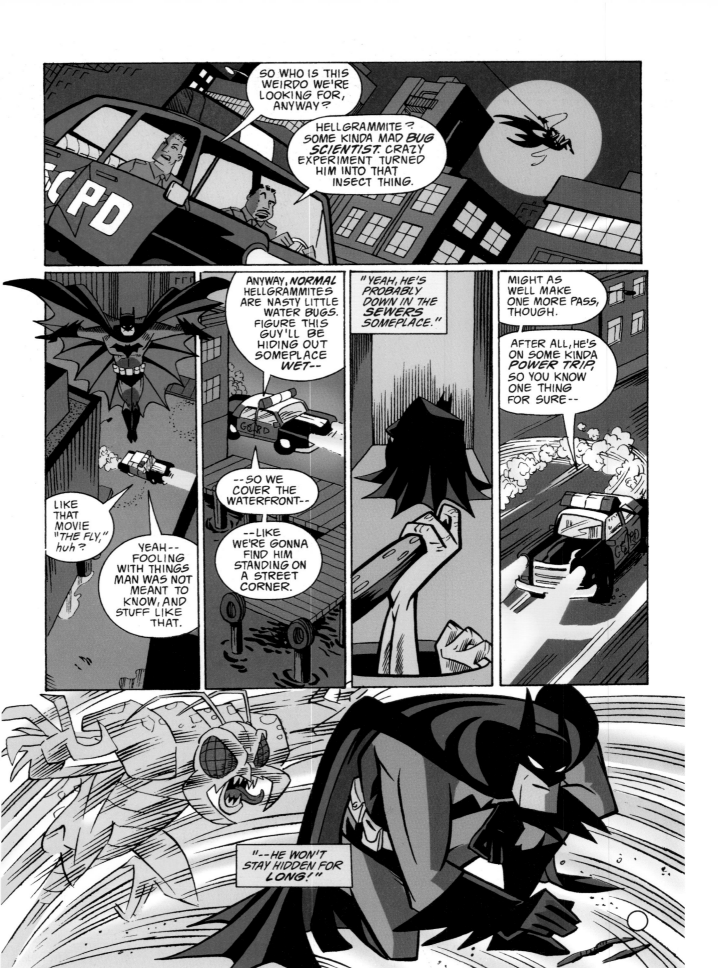

17

I'VE GOT A SPECIAL SQUAD ON THE WAY. THEY'LL GO DOWN THERE AND--

NO. THE SEWERS ARE HELLGRAMMITE'S TURF. IT'S TOO DANGEROUS.

BUT I CAN'T JUST LET HIM--

LEAVE HIM TO ME.

WHAT? BATMAN'S LEAVING-- HE'S NOT GOING AFTER HELLGRAMMITE!

MAYBE HE'S AFRAID-- MAYBE HE'S NOT AS HEROIC AS I THOUGHT!

I WISH I COULD HAVE HEARD WHAT HE AND GORDON WERE TALKING ABOUT!

EITHER I GO AFTER BATMAN AND THE SCOOP THAT WILL SAVE MY JOB--

--OR THE CREEPER GOES AFTER HELLGRAMMITE AND TRIES TO SAVE THE CITY!

SOME CHOICE!

GOT TO MOVE FAST, WHILE THE TRAIL IS FRESH!

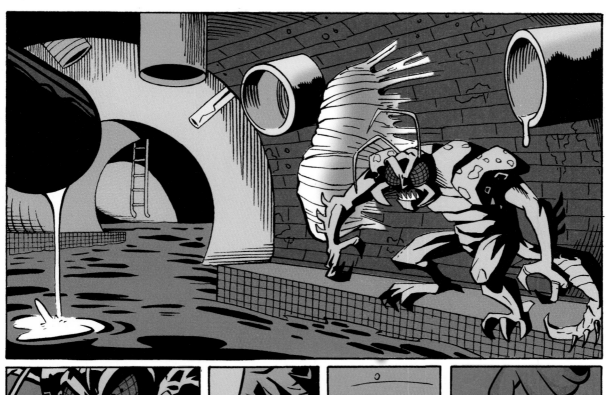

DRIP! DRIP!

HEY, BUG-BRAIN--!

BUT JUDGING FROM YOU, THEIR *EGOS* CAN GET PRETTY BLOATED!

WHAT MAKES YOU THINK *YOU* KNOW WHAT'S BEST FOR THE *WHOLE WORLD*?

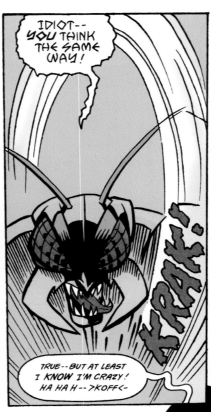

IDIOT-- *YOU* THINK THE SAME WAY!

KRAK!

TRUE--BUT AT LEAST I KNOW I'M CRAZY! HA HA H-->KOFF<

I'LL SHUT YOU UP FOR GOOD, YOU--

THWIP!

YOU! BUT HOW--?!

23

KLAANNG!

RRRRIPP!

PREEESENTING -- THAT SENSATIONAL SUPER-HERO TEAM-UP -- BATMAN AND BATTY MAN!

KRRUNCH!

YESSIR, I GOT 'IM ON THE ROPES NOW! ALL YOU GOTTA DO IS FINISH HIM OFF, BATMAN!

ah... BATMAN?

THE END

28

KILLER CROC'S CODED MESSAGE

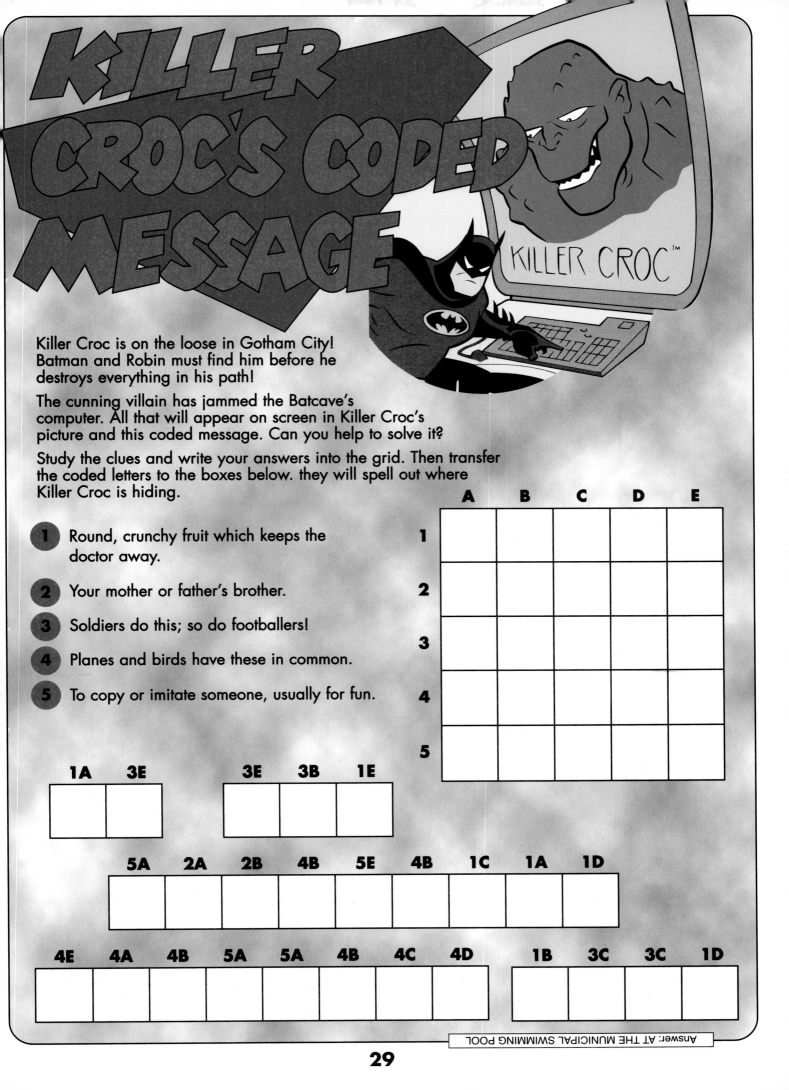

KILLER CROC™

Killer Croc is on the loose in Gotham City! Batman and Robin must find him before he destroys everything in his path!

The cunning villain has jammed the Batcave's computer. All that will appear on screen in Killer Croc's picture and this coded message. Can you help to solve it?

Study the clues and write your answers into the grid. Then transfer the coded letters to the boxes below. they will spell out where Killer Croc is hiding.

	A	B	C	D	E
1					
2					
3					
4					
5					

1 Round, crunchy fruit which keeps the doctor away.

2 Your mother or father's brother.

3 Soldiers do this; so do footballers!

4 Planes and birds have these in common.

5 To copy or imitate someone, usually for fun.

1A	3E		3E	3B	1E

5A	2A	2B	4B	5E	4B	1C	1A	1D

4E	4A	4B	5A	5A	4B	4C	4D		1B	3C	3C	1D

Answer: AT THE MUNICIPAL SWIMMING POOL

29

32

33

34

39

SUPERMAN'S TRANSATLANTIC ASSIGNMENT

Superman's alter ego, Clark Kent is a mild-mannered reporter on the Daily Planet newspaper. His editor has sent him to London on a special assignment and Clark will be working in the offices of a famous British newspaper. But which one?

Find out by solving this puzzle. The last letters of the American words on the left are also the first letters of the English words on the right. Fill in the missing letters and then the middle section, reading downwards, will spell the paper's name.

F	A	U	C	E		E	N	N	I	S	
	M	A	T			O	U	S	E		
C	O	O	K	I		G	G	S			
	H	O	O			R	A	U	G	H	T
	P	A	R	K		U	N	T			
	M	I	N			N	K	L	I	N	G
	F	A	L			O	T	T	E	R	Y
	C	A	N	D		A	C	H	T		
A	P	A	R	T	M	E	N		O	E	S
	G	A	S	O	L	I	N		X	P	O	R	T
	M	A	L			A	N	T	E	R	N
	A	I	R	P	L	A	N		N	E	R	G	Y
	P	I	T	C	H	I	N		O	A	L
	D	I	A	P	E		A	B	B	I	T
	Q	U	O	T		L	L	O	Y		
F	L	O	O	R	L	A	M		A	T	T	E	R	N
C	O	R	N	S	T	A	R	C		I	N	G

THE RIDDLERS DEADLY DOUBLE RIDDLE PUZZLE

Batman and Robin face a tricky situation - the Riddler has placed demolition charges under Gotham City Town Hall and they will go off in five minutes unless his riddles are solved. Can you help?

there are five short riddles which have to be solved. Each pair of lines will give you a letter. Put the letters together to make a word. Then put the word together to make another riddle.

No solution is given to the second riddle - you have to work it out for yourself! And remember to keep your eye on the time. You only have five minutes! So get going - and good luck!

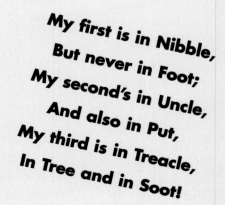

My first is in Whale,
In Where and in Who;
My second's in House,
But never in Blue;
My third is in Apple
And also in Ape;
My fourth is in Train,
And also in Tape!

My first is in Nibble,
But never in Foot;
My second's in Uncle,
And also in Put,
My third is in Treacle,
In Tree and in Soot!

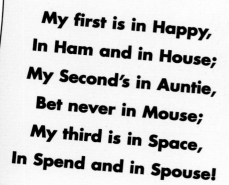

My first is in Happy,
In Ham and in House;
My Second's in Auntie,
Bet never in Mouse;
My third is in Space,
In Spend and in Spouse!

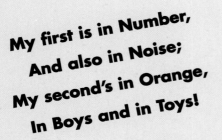

My first is in Number,
And also in Noise;
My second's in Orange,
In Boys and in Toys!

My first is in Shape,
And also in Shell;
My second's in Hampster,
But never in Bell;
My third is in Egg,
In Nose and in Eel;
My fourth is in Leg
And also in Reel;
My fifth is in Lie,
In Line and in Feel

Put together, these five words make this second riddle:

_ _ _ _   _ _ _   _ _ _   _ _   _ _ _ _ _ ?

GOOD AFTERNOON, LADIES AND GENTLEMEN-- THIS IS YOUR CAPTAIN SPEAKING. WE'LL BE ON THE GROUND IN KEYSTONE CITY IN--

HOLY SMOKES!

THEY'RE COMING RIGHT AT US! WE'RE GONNA CRASH!

LOOK--

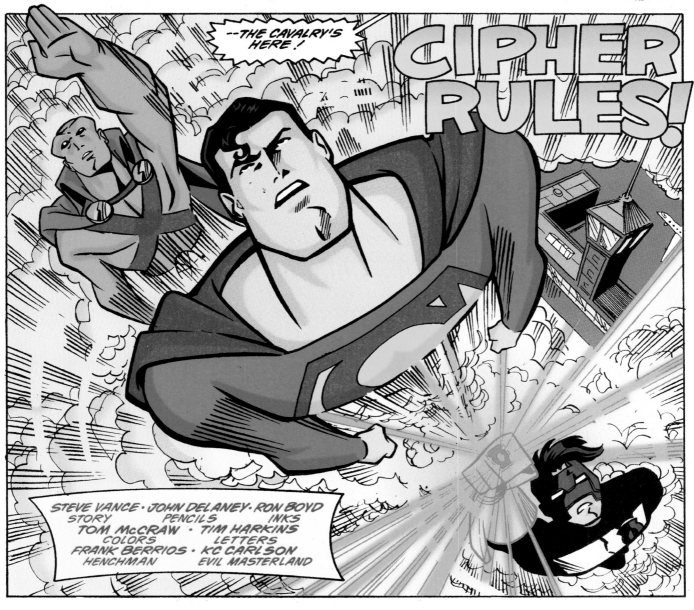

--THE CAVALRY'S HERE!

CIPHER RULES!

STEVE VANCE · JOHN DELANEY · RON BOYD
STORY   PENCILS   INKS
TOM McCRAW · TIM HARKINS
COLORS   LETTERS
FRANK BERRIOS · KC CARLSON
HENCHMAN   EVIL MASTERLAND

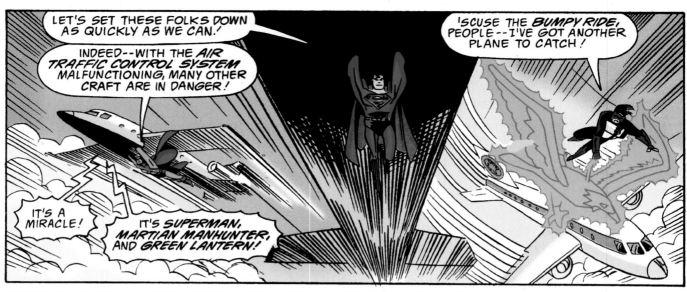

LET'S SET THESE FOLKS DOWN AS QUICKLY AS WE CAN!

INDEED--WITH THE AIR TRAFFIC CONTROL SYSTEM MALFUNCTIONING, MANY OTHER CRAFT ARE IN DANGER!

'SCUSE THE BUMPY RIDE, PEOPLE--I'VE GOT ANOTHER PLANE TO CATCH!

IT'S A MIRACLE!

IT'S SUPERMAN, MARTIAN MANHUNTER, AND GREEN LANTERN!

A HECTIC HALF HOUR LATER...

THANK YOU FOR FLYING AIR LANTERN --JUST DON'T BLAME ME IF YOUR LUGGAGE GOT LOST!

THAT'S THE LAST OF 'EM, GUYS-- GOOD WORK!

I GOTTA ADMIT-- THIS IS ONE TIME I WOULD'VE TRADED MY SUPER-SPEED FOR THE ABILITY TO FLY!

DON'T SWEAT IT, FLASH-- YOU MAY STILL GROW UP TO BE A REAL HERO ONE OF THESE DAYS.

LOOK WHO'S TALKING.

YOUR ABILITY TO TRACK ALL THE PLANES IN THE AREA SIMULTANEOUSLY WAS INVALUABLE, WALLY.

YOU DID THE JOB OF A WHOLE CREW OF FLIGHT CONTROLLERS. SPEAKING OF WHICH--

"--LET'S SEE IF THE FOLKS IN THE TOWER CAN EXPLAIN WHAT WENT WRONG!"

I WISH I KNEW! ONE MINUTE EVERYTHING WAS FINE -- THE NEXT, PHHT! OUR NEW G.P.S.* DATA LINK WENT HAYWIRE!

AT LEAST WE'RE BACK ON-LINE NOW!

WOW--WE GOT HALF THE JLA HERE! COULD I GET YOUR AUTOGRAPHS?

*GLOBAL POSITIONING SATELLITE --KC

46

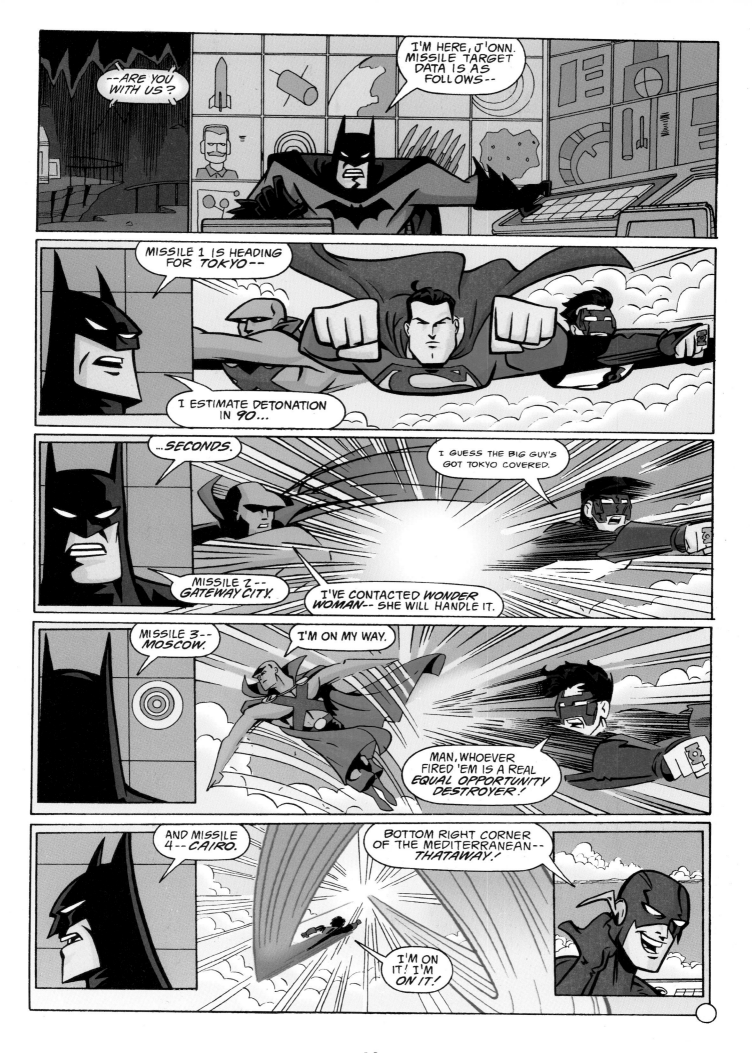

--NOW!

WHOOMPF!

WHEW!

NICE SAFE--ER, SAVE, KYLE.

THANKS.

NOW THAT I'VE *GOT IT*, WHAT DO I *DO WITH IT*?

ALLOW ME.

I'LL JUST TOSS IT OUT OF *EARTH'S GRAVITY WELL* AND LET IT FALL HARMLESSLY INTO THE SUN, AS I DID WITH THE OTHER MISSILES.

NOW LET'S SEE ABOUT THAT *SUBMARINE*...

NOT TO WORRY, SUPERMAN--

--THAT'S BEEN *TAKEN CARE OF.*

I'LL MAKE SURE THE CREW GETS PICKED UP BY A NICE, SMELLY *TRAMP STEAMER*--

--AS SOON AS I'M DONE *QUESTIONING THE CAPTAIN.*

≈KAFFKAFF≈ I'LL TALK!

THE SUB COMMANDER SAYS HE RECEIVED *AUTHENTICATED* ORDERS. I THINK HE'S TELLING THE TRUTH.

I'VE GOT THE *LUNVANIAN* PREMIER ON THE LINE-- HE *DENIES* ORDERING THE SUB TO LAUNCH MISSILES.

SO ONE OF THEM IS *LYING* --

--OR *SOMEONE ELSE* HAS GAINED CONTROL OF THEIR *COMMUNICATIONS SYSTEM!*

VERY ASTUTE, *MANHUNTER!* IT IS *MY* FINGER ON THE *NUCLEAR BUTTON!*

I'VE BEEN EAVESDROPPING ON *FLASH'S* PHONE CALL-- I COULDN'T HELP OVERHEARING YOUR COMMENT!

WHO THE --?

ALLOW ME TO INTRODUCE MYSELF. I AM *CIPHER* --

--EARTH'S *NEW MASTER!*

IT WAS I WHO DISRUPTED *KEYSTONE'S* AIR TRAFFIC CONTROL. I HAVE SEIZED CONTROL OF ALL GLOBAL *TELECOMMUNICATIONS* --

WHERE'S *KENT?!* THE STORY OF THE YEAR, AND HE'S *MISSING* IT!

--JUST AS I NOW CONTROL THE ENTIRE *LUNVANIAN* NUCLEAR SUBMARINE FLEET!

MY FIRST ORDER TO YOU, MY NEW *SLAVES,* IS --

--THE SURRENDER OF THE JLA!

LIKE FUN.

IF YOU REFUSE, I WILL LAUNCH THE ENTIRE LUNVANIAN NUCLEAR ARSENAL!

ADMIT THAT YOU ARE HELPLESS BEFORE MY POWER--

--OR YOU SO-CALLED HEROES WILL BE RESPONSIBLE FOR THE INCINERATION OF THE PLANET!

YOU HAVE ONE HOUR TO DECIDE!

GEEZ-- HE'S A GREAT CONVERSATIONALIST, ISN'T HE?

BATMAN-- WHAT ARE WE UP AGAINST?

28 M-CLASS SUBS --24 ICBMS PER SUB, EACH WITH 12 WARHEADS. THAT'S--

I KNOW, I KNOW--A BUNCH--!

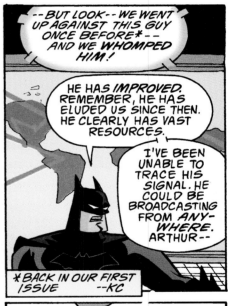

--BUT LOOK-- WE WENT UP AGAINST THIS GUY ONCE BEFORE*-- AND WE WHOMPED HIM!

HE HAS IMPROVED. REMEMBER, HE HAS ELUDED US SINCE THEN. HE CLEARLY HAS VAST RESOURCES.

I'VE BEEN UNABLE TO TRACE HIS SIGNAL. HE COULD BE BROADCASTING FROM ANY-WHERE. ARTHUR--

*BACK IN OUR FIRST ISSUE --KC

--CAN YOU LOCATE THOSE SUBS IN TIME?

NOT A CHANCE. I SUSPECT I ONLY FOUND THE FIRST ONE BECAUSE CIPHER WANTED ME TO.

WE'VE GOTTA AT LEAST TRY TO FIND HIM!

I CAN COVER A LOT OF GROUND IN AN HOUR--

LOOK--

--I DON'T THINK WE HAVE AN HOUR.

--RIOTING HAS BROKEN OUT IN MAJOR CITIES AROUND THE GLOBE--

--AS PANICKED CITIZENS ATTEMPT TO FLEE METROPOLITAN AREAS IN THE WAKE OF CIPHER'S THREATS.

AND NOW, A MESSAGE FROM OUR NETWORK'S CHAIRMAN, WINSTON MCKINNEY!

ORDINARILY, I PREFER TO WORK *BEHIND THE SCENES*-- AWAY FROM THE SPOTLIGHT-- BUT IN THIS MOMENT OF CRISIS, I MUST MAKE MY VOICE HEARD.

I URGE THE JLA TO PROVE THAT THEY ARE MORE THAN GLORY-SEEKING *VIGILANTES* BY SURRENDERING TO CIPHER FOR THE SAKE OF ALL MANKIND.

MEANWHILE, THE REST OF US MUST NOT PANIC.

I, ALONG WITH MY ENTIRE STAFF OF DEVOTED EMPLOYEES, WILL BE CARRYING ON BUSINESS AS USUAL RIGHT TO THE END. I CALL ON EVERYONE ELSE TO DO LIKEWISE.

THANK YOU.

RRRING!

GADSDEN GRAVES HERE.

WHAT *IS* IT, MARTHA?

MR. MCKINNEY *TAPED* THAT ANNOUNCEMENT AND LEFT IN SUCH A HURRY-- AND I KNOW YOU'RE IN CHARGE WHILE HE'S GONE, SO I THOUGHT YOU SHOULD KNOW--

WE-WE'VE LOST CONTACT WITH HIS *HELICOPTER!* YOU KNOW, HE WAS ON HIS WAY TO HIS PRIVATE *FALLOUT SHELTER,* AND--

CALM DOWN, MARTHA --IT'S JUST A COMMUNICATIONS GLITCH DUE TO THIS *CIPHER* LUNATIC--

--I HOPE.

IF THAT CREEP MCKINNEY WANTS US TO SURRENDER, IT *CAN'T* BE THE RIGHT THING.

MAYBE CIPHER'S *BLUFFING!*

ARE WE PREPARED TO TAKE THAT RISK?

AND I THOUGHT *OUR* JOB WAS A HEAVY BURDEN.

WHAT DO *THEY* HAVE TO WORRY ABOUT? NUKES JUST BOUNCE OFF THAT CREW!

SOME OF THEM AREN'T EVEN *FROM* EARTH-- WHAT DO *THEY* CARE WHAT HAPPENS TO *US?*

THEY CAN JUST FLY OFF AND FIND A *NEW* PLANET.

THEY'VE *GOT* TO CARE. THEY'RE OUR *ONLY* HOPE!

50 MINUTES... STACY WILL BE ON HER WAY HOME FROM SCHOOL...

55

-- SO AT THIS MOMENT, THE *JUSTICE LEAGUE* IS ASSEMBLING AT AN UNDISCLOSED LOCATION, WHERE THEY WILL SURRENDER TO CIPHER.

TURN OFF THE TV AND GET READY!

I--I'M KINDA NERVOUS. THIS IS THE FIRST TIME I'VE BEEN FACE TO FACE WITH THESE SUPER-GUYS.

THERE'S NOTHING TO WORRY ABOUT. AS LONG AS THE BOSS HAS HIS FINGER ON THE BUTTON, THOSE GUYS DON'T DARE EVEN *LOOK* AT US FUNNY.

I-I GUESS SO.

RELAX! JUST ACT CONFIDENT. REMEMBER, YOU'RE ON THE WINNING SIDE-- PART OF THE TEAM THAT FINALLY *BEAT THE JLA!*

TELEPORTER'S FIRING UP--!

VRRRRRRRZZZ ZZZZ

THEY'RE *HERE!*

ZZZ-O-AAAA-AAKK!

ALL RIGHT, TOUGH GUYS -- LET'S GO! WE'VE GOT *VERY SPECIAL CELLS* WAITING FOR YOU!

RELAX... CONFIDENT... WINNING SIDE... RELAX... CONFIDENT... WINNING SIDE...

RELAX... CONFIDENT... WINNING SIDE... DON'T DARE LOOK AT US FUNNY...

BOO.

ZIP!

58

ANY LUCK, J'ONN?

NONE, BATMAN.

THE ENERGY FIELDS SURROUNDING CIPHER'S LAIR ARE DISRUPTING MY TELEPATHIC PROBES.

WE'VE GOT TO DEVISE AN *ESCAPE PLAN* -- BEFORE THAT *MADMAN* DECIDES TO THROW A FEW *NUKES* JUST FOR FUN!

WE'LL HAVE TO STRIKE FAST -- TAKE HIM BY SURPRISE. FIRST, WE NEED TO FIGURE OUT THE LAYOUT OF THIS COMPLEX --

HEY, BATMAN -- I'VE GOT AN IDEA. NOT ONLY THAT --

-- I'VE GOT MY *RING!* THE ONE I GAVE THE GUARD WAS A RING-CONSTRUCT. I PALMED MY REAL ONE.

ANYWAY, HERE'S MY PLAN...

LOOK AT 'EM -- THE MIGHTY *JUSTICE LEAGUE!* THEY'RE NOT SO TOUGH NOW, HUH?

CHECK OUT THE *FASTEST MAN ALIVE* --

-- JUST *STANDING THERE!* THAT CELL'S LINED WITH A COUNTER-VIBRATIONAL ALLOY -- HE KNOWS HE CAN'T GET OUT!

OH NO! *LOOK!* MARTIAN MANHUNTER'S GONE!

HE'S *ESCAPED!* CIPHER'LL KILL ME! I'LL CHECK HIS CELL-- YOU GO GET *HELP*--

DON'T BE A *SUCKER*-- HE DIDN'T ESCAPE! HE CAN *TURN INVISIBLE!* SEE-- SENSORS ARE STILL READING HIS HEARTBEAT AND RESPIRATION!

HE'S *STILL IN THERE,* WAITING FOR YOU TO OPEN THE DOOR AND LOOK FOR HIM! THEN HE'LL SLUG YOU AND WALTZ OUT! OLDEST TRICK IN THE BOOK.

WATCH! I'LL JUST TURN ON THE *FLAME JETS* BUILT INTO THE WALLS OF HIS CELL. WATCH HOW FAST HE TURNS VISIBUHH--

ahh-- NICE, CLEARLY MARKED CONTROLS! I WOULD'VE HATED TO ACCIDENTALLY TURN ON THE *KRYPTONITE GAS* INSTEAD OF OPENING THE DOORS.

WHOK!

THOK!

WELL DONE, WALLY.

THANKS FOR THE *DIVERSION,* J'ONN. ONCE *GL* GOT MY *CELL DOOR UNLOCKED,* THE REST WAS EASY.

TO MAKE SURE THE VIDEO CAMERA COULDN'T DETECT MY ABSENCE, I HAD TO KEEP MY *SCOUTING TRIPS* SHORTER THAN *1/30TH* OF A SECOND.

THAT'S WHY IT TOOK ME ALMOST *TWO SECONDS* TO COVER THE WHOLE COMPLEX!

COME ON -- CIPHER'S LAIR IS THIS WAY!

SO THE JLA ESCAPED FROM THEIR CELLS-- HOW VERY *RESOURCEFUL* OF THEM!

PERHAPS THEY CAN *STILL* PROVIDE ME WITH A BIT OF ENTERTAINMENT!

THERE! YOU CAN'T STOP IT NOW--

--MY TARGETING COMPUTER'S SIGNAL HAS GONE OUT THROUGH THE SATELLITE UPLINK ANTENNA! IN SECONDS, MISSILES WILL BE--

TARGETING COMPUTER? UPLINK ANTENNA?

--OH, DO YOU MEAN THESE? I'M AFRAID THEY'RE EXPERIENCING TECHNICAL DIFFICULTIES RIGHT NOW, CIPHER.

WHAT?!

YOU-YOU TRICKED ME! YOU CHEATED! AND YOU CALL YOURSELVES HEROES!

NICE WORK, J'ONN!

AN HONOR, SUPERMAN. SHALL WE..?

ALL RIGHT, CIPHER! YOUR GAME IS--

KA-THOOOM!

HA! I KNEW CAPTURING THAT *ARROGANT WINDBAG* WAS A GOOD IDEA!

HE'S THE PERFECT *FALL GUY* TO SUCKER THE JLA!

THEIR SHAPE-SHIFTING MARTIAN MAY HAVE FOOLED *ME*--

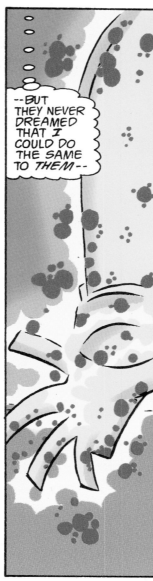

--BUT THEY NEVER DREAMED THAT *I* COULD DO THE SAME TO *THEM*--

--THANKS TO MY HOLOGRAM-PROJECTING *BODY HARNESS!*

I'LL *TELEPORT* OUT OF HERE--

--AND THEY'LL NEVER *KNOW*--

≡OOOF!≡

WE'RE NOT LED ASTRAY *THAT* EASILY, CIPHER. OR SHOULD I CALL YOU--

TRAITOR!

HOW COULD YOU DO THIS TO ME? YOU SET ME *UP!* YOU *BETRAYED* ME! YOU MIGHT HAVE *KILLED* ME!

65

MY OWN RIGHT-HAND MAN-- GADSDEN GRAVES!

I BETRAYED YOU?!

IT WAS *MY GENIUS* THAT *BUILT* YOUR COMPANY! YOU TOOK ME FOR GRANTED --BELITTLED ME-- USED ME--AND *YOU* GOT ALL THE *GLORY!*

I WANTED TO SHOW THE WORLD THAT *I* WAS A BIG MAN, TOO-- *BIGGER* THAN *YOU!*

I USED THE WEAPONS, THE SATELLITES, THE COMMUNICATIONS SYSTEMS THAT I DESIGNED-- THAT MADE YOU RICH -- TO BECOME *CIPHER!*

YOU LEFT ME TO OVERSEE CONSTRUCTION OF YOUR PERSONAL BOMB SHELTER --SO I BUILT *THIS* INSTEAD!

I HAD MORE POWER THAN YOU CAN EVEN *IMAGINE*--BUT SOMETHING WAS MISSING.

THIS!

THIS IS WHAT I WANTED ALL ALONG-- THE CHANCE TO TELL YOU THAT YOU'RE *THROUGH!*

I *STOLE* McKINNEY BROADCASTING'S *LAST PENNY* TO FINANCE MY OPERATIONS! YOU'RE *BROKE! RUINED! BANKRUPT!*

WH-WHAT?

BROKE?

WE SAVE THE WORLD FROM *NUCLEAR INCINERATION* AND ALL HE CAN THINK ABOUT IS THE FACT THAT HE'S *STRAPPED FOR CASH!*

YEAH. WELL, LET ME TELL YOU--

"--IT COULDN'T HAVE HAPPENED TO A NICER GUY."

END

THE JOKERS
CODED JOKE PUZZLE

Batman needs help again - urgently! This time, the Joker is holding Gotham City to ransom. He has hacked his way into the Municipal Computer System and can transfer the City's money into his own account!

Being the Joker, of course, he has provided a cunning get-out in the form of a coded joke. You have to:

1. **Crack the code (clue given)**
2. **Write out the joke**
3. **Think of the punchline (clue given)**
4. **Complete the second code**
5. **Turn the punchline into a number sequence**

Only then will the City's Computer have the correct combination to deny the Joker access!

Here is the Joker's coded joke...
(You'll be a bit backward if you don't crack it!)

TAHW SI NEPO NEHW TI SI DESOLC DNA DESOLC NEHW TI SI NEPO?

Written properly, the joke reads...

_ _ _ _   _ _   _ _ _ _   _ _ _ _   _ _   _ _   _ _ _ _ _ _

_ _ _   _ _ _ _ _ _   _ _ _ _   _ _   _ _   _ _ _ _   _ _

The punchline is...
(famous London Landmark) _ _ _ _ _   _ _ _ _ _ _

Now complete the second code...   A – 1, B – 2, C – 3, etc...

And convert the punchline into numbers... _ _ _ _ _   _ _ _ _ _ _

SINCE I CAN RUN *AROUND THE GLOBE* IN A *MILLI SECOND*, I DON'T OFTEN TAKE *PLANES*.

SO, THIS WASN'T *MY* IDEA.

IT'S A *VACATION!* WE'LL HAVE A NICE RELAXING FLIGHT TOGETHER--

DID I MENTION OUR *FOUR-HOUR* DELAY IN *GATEWAY CITY*? THE ONE THAT LOST HALF OUR *BAGS*?

--AND ARRIVE *RESTED* AND *READY* TO ENJOY SOME FUN IN THE SUN!

SUUUURE.

SORRY TO DISAPPOINT, FOLKS, BUT THIS IS JUST A *VACATION!*

HOW DOES *SUPERBOY* FEEL ABOUT YOU ENCROACHING ON HIS TURF?

oh, BROTHER...

TAXI!

THE SO-CALLED "*FASTEST MAN ALIVE,*" REFUSED TO DIVULGE THE *PURPOSE* OF HIS *SECRET MISSION*--

Gaaah! THESE ARE DAYS WHEN I *WISH* I STILL HAD A *SECRET IDENTITY!*

--BUT IT SEEMS SAFE TO SAY THAT HAWAII SHOULD BE PREPARED FOR SOME *UNIVERSE-RATTLING MENACES*--

DID I SAY "DAYS"? I MEANT *DECADES!*

LINDA, THIS IS *INSANE!*

WALLY!, WHAT'S *INSANE* IS *YOU* WATCHING TV WHEN IT'S *80°* OUTSIDE!

WE'RE HERE TO ESCAPE THE *MIDWESTERN WINTER*, REMEMBER? LET'S HIT THE *BEACH!*

HEY!

KLIK!

WHATEVER THE *MYSTERY* THREAT MAY BE--*

...MAY BE, IS IT SO BIG THAT THE MAINLAND SPEEDSTER FEARS OUR OWN *SUPERBOY* IS INCAPABLE OF FACING IT ALONE?

KLIK!

I THINK I'M GONNA BE *SICK!*

70

73

PWOOOOSH!

THE PRESSURE'S ESCAPING! YOU DID IT, S.B.!

WOW-- I SURE DID!

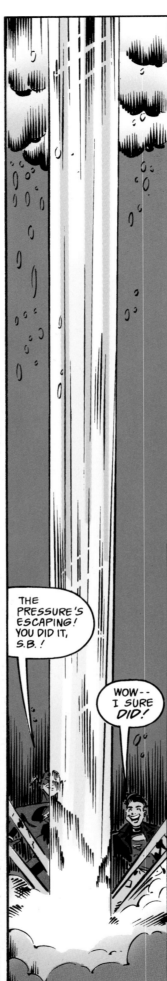

SO WHADDAYA SAY-- SHALL WE GET BACK TO THE RACE?

aw, WHAT'S THE POINT? YOU COULD OUTRUN ME WITH NINE TOES TIED BEHIND YOUR BACK.

THOSE REPORTERS 'LL SAY I'M FULL OF HOT AIR-- LIKE MAUNA KEA.

AND THEY'LL BE RIGHT.

KID, IF THERE'S ONE THING I'VE LEARNED IN THIS BUSINESS, IT'S THAT YOU CAN'T WORRY ABOUT YOUR PRESS CLIPPINGS.

JUST LISTEN TO YOUR HEAD-- AND YOUR HEART. IF YOU KNOW YOU DID THE BEST YOU COULD, THAT'S WHAT COUNTS.

NOW COME ON! IT'S TIME FOR A LITTLE ... FANCY FOOTWORK!

HERE THEY COME! THEY'RE NECK AND NECK!

--IT'S GOING TO BE A PHOTO FINISH! WHAT A STORY!

F I N I S H

OKAY, SUPERBOY--

--LET'S BUST SOME DUST!

Z-OOOOM

I AM THE SPEED KING.

NO, I AM.

NO, ME!

WHAT COULD YOU SEE--?

NOT A THING.

IS THIS SOME KIND OF COVER-UP? THE PUBLIC HAS A RIGHT TO KNOW WHO WON!

HEY, WITH ALL THOSE CAMERAS, I'M SURE YOU GOT PLENTY OF FABULOUS PICTURES!

SORRY IF YOU MISSED THE PHOTO OP OF THE CENTURY, GUYS--

--BUT WE BOTH KNOW WHO'S THE FASTEST MAN ALIVE, DON'T WE?

YOU GOT THAT RIGHT, SUPERBOY!

SUPER-SIZE SUPERMAN SPOT THE DIFFERENCE

There is a total of *15 differences* between these two pictures of Superman in front of the Gotham City skyline. Some are obvious and easy to spot; others are smaller and harder to find.

Can you see them all?

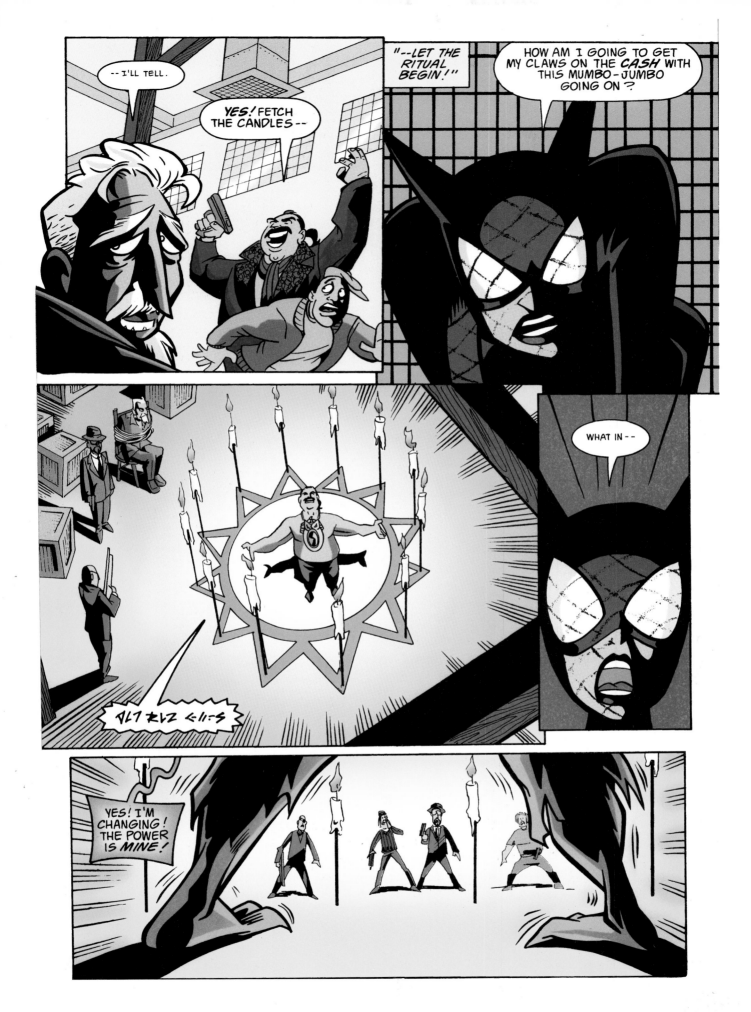

93

WHOK!

THAT WAS HARDLY EVEN A WORKOUT!

NOW TO GET THIS THING BACK TO *WONDER WOMAN.*

I MUST BE *CRAZY,* JUMPING OUT OF THE FRYING PAN, INTO THE FIRE -- AND *BACK AGAIN!*

PLEASE -- DON'T LEAVE ME TIED UP!

Oh, WHAT THE HECK.

SSSLICE!

NEXT I'LL BE HELPING LITTLE OLD LADIES CROSS THE STREET!

HOLD THAT POSE, GODZILLA!

CATWOMAN! SO YOU'RE IN A HURRY TO *DIE*, EH?

I'LL BE HAPPY TO OBLIGE!

SORRY, BRAGG--

--BUT I'M NOT INTERESTED IN A CAT FIGHT WITH YOU.

SHE HAS RETURNED-- AND NOW SHE RISKS HER LIFE TO AID ME!

BRAGG!

PROF. FULLER--WE MET AT THE ARCHAEOLOGICAL CONFERENCE! DO YOU KNOW THIS MAN?

HE KIDNAPPED ME-- BUT CATWOMAN FREED ME.

CATWOMAN--?

ANOTHER UNEXPECTED GOOD DEED.

THE POOR FOOL. IS HE--?

UNCONSCIOUS.

AS THE GODS OF ANCIENT GREECE DREW THEIR POWERS FROM THE BELIEF OF THEIR FOLLOWERS--

I AM NOTHING-- NOBODY.

--HE DREW HIS FROM A BELIEF IN HIS OWN SUPERIORITY.

AND YOU MADE HIM LOOK WITHIN-- SHATTERING THAT BELIEF.

108

THE DYNAMIC DUO'S DEADLY WEAPONS SPIRAL

As they do not possess any superpowers, Batman and Robin sometimes resort to using their Bat-weapons to overcome their enemies.

To find out some of the items in their secret arsenal, solve this puzzle. Read each clue and work out what sort of weapon is being indicated.

Then write the names of each weapon into the spiral grid, remembering that the last letter of one weapon is also the first letter of the next.

1. Long-bladed weapon kept in a scabbard

2. Short, sharp-pointed knife - often hidden and used for stabbing

3. Handgun with turning mechanism often used by cowboys

4. Powerful flying weapon, and means of transport in Space

5. Small hand axe used by native Americans

6. Worn on the hand to give extra power to punches

7. Used for battering down doors

8. Modern weapon fired from a launcher and often laser-guided

Answer:
1. SWORD
2. DAGGER
3. REVOLVER
4. ROCKET
5. TOMAHAWK
6. KNUCKLEDUSTER
7. RAM
8. MISSILE